THE WORLD TURNED UPSIDE DOWN

UPSIDE DOWN

CHILDREN OF 1776

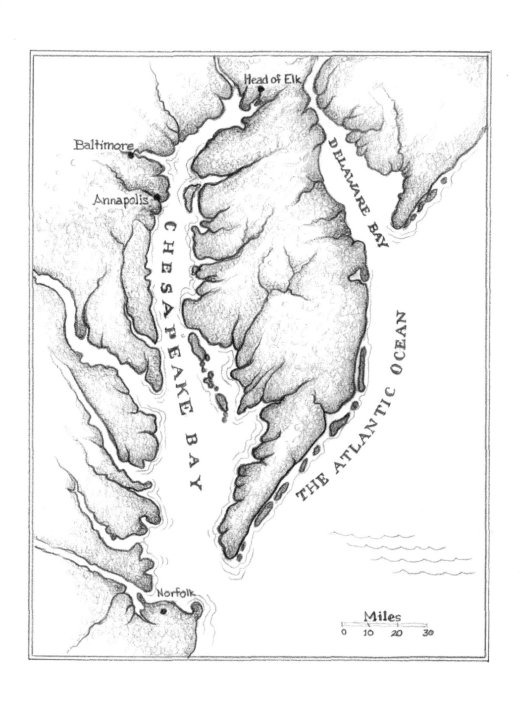

Head of Elk

Baltimore

Annapolis

DELAWARE BAY

C H E S A P E A K E   B A Y

THE ATLANTIC OCEAN

Norfolk

Miles

0   10   20   30

THE WORLD TURNED UPSIDE DOWN
CHILDREN OF 1776

by
ANN JENSEN

illustrated by
MARCY DUNN RAMSEY

Tidewater Publishers
Centreville, Maryland

Library of Congress Cataloging-in-Publication Data

Jensen, Ann, 1940–
    The world turned upside down : children of 1776 / by Ann Jensen.—1st ed.
        p. cm.
    Includes index.
    ISBN 0-87033-534-0 (pbk.)
    1. Annapolis (Md.)—History—18th century—Juvenile literature. 2. Sands
family—Juvenile literature. 3. Maryland—History—Revolution, 1775–1783—Juvenile
literature. [1. Annapolis (Md.)—History—18th century. 2. Sands family. 3.
Maryland—History—Revolution, 1775–1783.] I. Title

F189.A657 J46 2001
975.2′56—dc21   2001023412

Manufactured in the United States of America
First edition, 2001; second printing, 2002

To Margaret Moss Dowsett and Frederick R. Dowsett; and to the memory of Jane Revell Moss and her sister, Margaret Revell, who loved and preserved the Sands House, its furnishings, and the family letters, diaries, and documents from which this story grew.

"*They're Burning the* Peggy Stewart!"

Only the Stewarts' tightly shuttered windows gave any sign that something was amiss that Tuesday morning in Annapolis in October 1774. Nan Sands's knock on the Stewarts' door brought a squawk from an angry mockingbird in a nearby maple tree, and then all was quiet on Hanover Street once more. Nan tried again, rapping so hard she had to rub her sore knuckles. Still no answer. She shifted her basket from her left arm to her right and stepped off the porch to look up at the house.

"Did one of the shutters move?" She stood quietly for a moment, looking and listening.

"Maybe they didn't hear," she thought.

"Maybe I imagined that the shutter moved."

"Or maybe the Stewarts have fled." Nan shook her head and went back up onto the porch. "No, Mrs. Stewart couldn't leave with her baby barely two days old."

As Nan raised her hand to knock once more, the door opened—but slowly, and only a crack. A slave woman peeked out at her.

"I have the coverlets and shirts Mrs. Stewart ordered," said Nan taking a bundle from her basket. She was fifteen and for two years had been earning extra money for her family with her sewing. When the birth of the Stewarts' baby drew near, Mrs. Stewart had ordered several small woolen blankets and tiny linen shirts from Nan.

"Yes'm, she says thank you," said the woman. She opened the door wide enough for a frightened look up and down the street, then took the bundle and handed Nan ten shillings. "The mistress says to go home quickly, child. It's not safe. There are dangerous men about. Go home!" And before Nan could say a word, the woman hastily closed the door.

Nan slipped the coins into the pocket beneath her apron as she turned and left. She looked one way and then the other, just as the slave woman had, and would not have been surprised to see an angry crowd come raging down the empty street. Instead, she heard a soft voice calling her name.

"Nan! Nan Sands, look up here!" Peering up through the thinning leaves of the maple tree, Nan saw Peggy Stewart leaning out of an upstairs window. Peggy looked fearfully up and down the street.

"A great crowd of men was here yesterday," she said in a loud whisper. "They were shouting for Father and throwing rocks at the house. We were very much afraid."

"Yes, I heard," said Nan, whispering also. "How is your mother? And the baby?"

"Mother is still abed," answered Peggy, and then, for a moment her face brightened. "I have a new sister. . . ."

Before she could say more, her brother James appeared beside her. "Come away from the window!" he said angrily and pulled Peggy back into the house.

Nan had time only to wave and call good-bye before Peggy disappeared and James slammed the window shut.

Sadly, Nan turned away from the Stewart house and hurried down Hanover Street. "'Tis a bad time to be born into that family," her mother had said when they heard that the Stewarts' baby had been born.

"It's not the best of times to be Peggy Stewart either," thought Nan. The brig that Peggy's father, Anthony Stewart, had named for her was at that moment under guard at the town dock. Ever since Saturday last when the *Peggy Stewart* sailed into the harbor with a load of tea, there had been nothing but trouble in Annapolis. Remembering that, Nan walked a little faster.

Rounding a bend in the path that would take her home from Hanover Street, Nan nearly collided with her brother Johnny. "Ma sent me to fetch you home," he said, turning to lead the way along the narrow path. "This is not the time to have dealings with the Stewarts. Men are gathering now at the dock. They're saying they will give Mr. Stewart a coat of tar and feathers. Do you think they will?" he asked, looking back over his shoulder at her.

"No, that is just a lot of hotheaded talk," said Nan, frowning at her younger brother. He was nearly thirteen and had been spending entirely too much time listening to the men in the public room of their parents' ordinary. "You heard Pa. He said the townsmen would never let that happen. And don't let Pa hear you saying such things." She was glad he couldn't see her face. She wasn't nearly as confident as she sounded.

Every night since Saturday, Nan had fallen asleep to the sound of angry voices in the public room below her bed chamber. She guessed that men had been gathering in every other inn and tavern in town to argue about what to do with Anthony Stewart, his ship, and the cargo of tea that was the cause of all the fuss.

Even before October 15 when the *Peggy Stewart* sailed into the Annapolis harbor, people in Maryland and the other colonies had been angry about tea. Actually, they were angry about how the government, far away in England, made laws for Americans and taxed things like tea without as much as a by-your-leave.

First Parliament had taxed molasses. Then it taxed paper, and finally in 1773 Parliament taxed tea. That was one tax too many. In December 1773, a group of men in Boston decided they had had enough of Parliament and its taxes and dumped three shiploads of tea into Boston harbor. In answer, Parliament punished the people of Boston by closing their port. Bostonians did much of their business and got most of their food and other necessities by boat, so closing their port was strong punishment.

Marylanders sent the people of Boston their sympathy and one thousand bushels of corn. During the spring of 1774 the most important men in the colony met to decide what to do until King George and Parliament were ready to respect the rights of Americans. One of the first things they decided was to send four Marylanders to the First Continental Congress in Philadelphia. Next they agreed not to import tea or other taxed goods from England. These decisions gave Annapolitans reason to be angry when the *Peggy Stewart* arrived from England with a load of tea. They were especially angry when Anthony Stewart paid the tax on it.

Nevertheless, many Annapolitans were willing to accept Anthony Stewart's apology for ordering the tea in the first place and then paying the hated tea tax. Others would have been satisfied to let him destroy the tea and be done with the whole thing. Saturday, October 15, however, was the worst possible time for the *Peggy Stewart* to have come to town with a load of tea. The law courts were in session, and Saturday was market day, one of the busiest days of the week. Annapolis was full of men from Baltimore and from farms and plantations around Anne Arundel County. They, and a few Annapolitans, were not content to allow Anthony Stewart simply to destroy the tea his ship carried. They wanted much stronger punishment than that, and no one could be sure that cool heads would decide Anthony Stewart's fate.

Nan wondered what would happen to Peggy Stewart and her family. She was relieved to be on her way home—and with ten shillings. She jingled the coins in her pocket. Johnny heard and looked back at her with a grin. "For a penny, I'll play you a tune," he said, and from his belt he pulled a small wooden fife that he had made.

"Not even a half-penny," said Nan. "I've heard you practicing."

Her brother was undaunted. "See if you can guess this tune," he said. He put the fife to his lips and began to play as they walked. Nan listened and then shook her head. "You'll never make a fifer," she said. "I can't guess."

He tried again. After a few more steps, she began to hum along. "Yes, I do know it," she said and began to sing the words to the little tune that was heard more and more around Annapolis those days.

If buttercups buzzed after the bee,
If boats were on land, churches on sea,
If ponies rode men and grass ate the cows
And cats should be chased to holes by the mouse,
If a mama sold her baby to gypsies for a crown,
If summer were spring and t'other way 'round,
Then all of the world would be turned upside down.

"A foolish bit of music," Nan thought, but if ever a song described how it was in Annapolis that autumn of 1774, it was "The World Turned Upside Down."

She hurried after her brother. One thing hadn't changed: she was needed at home to help with the midday meal. Nan was certain that more than the usual three or four travelers and workmen would soon be crowding into the Sands ordinary and that they would be hungry for their dinner and thirsty from all their arguing about the fate of the *Peggy Stewart*.

By the next morning, October 19, the arguments had ended. The hotter heads had decided what to do about the *Peggy Stewart* and her cargo of tea. Cries spread through the streets of Annapolis like fire in dry tinder.

"They're burning the *Peggy Stewart!*"

Chores forgotten, Johnny Sands ran toward the Severn River's shore where a crowd had gathered. There, he found his brother Will who had been hunting upriver for small game and wildfowl since before dawn.

"Take this," said Will. He handed Johnny the game bag he was carrying. "The hunting was good this morning."

"I can feel that," said Johnny, grunting as he swung the heavy bag over his shoulder. He wished that Will had let him carry his flintlock gun instead. He was about to say as much, but Will was already trotting down toward the water's edge. Johnny had to run to catch up. Ahead, he could see the *Peggy Stewart*. She was under full sail but already had gone aground in the shallows off Windmill Point. From where he and Will stood, Johnny saw several men scramble over the brig's side and into a waiting skiff. Before the little boat was away from the *Peggy Stewart*'s side,

black smoke was billowing from her hold. Some in the crowd cheered at the sight.

"Look," said Johnny. He pointed to the small boat that was pulling away from the *Peggy Stewart*. "It's Mr. Stewart in the skiff. He set fire to her himself."

"Aye," said Will. "He had no choice. It was that or his hide."

As flames began to lick at the brig's sails, Johnny looked back over his shoulder and saw his father, John Sands, pushing through the crowd toward them. Johnny recognized the stormy look on his father's face. Like many other Annapolitans, John Sands had argued against destroying the *Peggy Stewart* after Anthony Stewart apologized and agreed to burn the tea.

"Come away. You've seen enough," he said to Johnny and Will. "We will not support this action with our presence."

John Sands turned his back on the river and the burning ship and headed for home. Will shook his head, scowled at his younger brother who was about to protest, and reluctantly the two boys followed their father.

"The World Turned Upside Down"

*W*hen the *Peggy Stewart* was a smoldering wreck, some Annapolitans felt better. Most did not. They were still angry with the government in England, and burning a shipload of tea did not change that. Just because they were an ocean away did not mean that people in Maryland or any other colony should not have the same privileges as the king's subjects in Great Britain. As angry as they were, most Annapolitans still wanted to be loyal to King George. They still felt that they were English. Wasn't Annapolis named for an English queen? Wasn't there a Fleet Street, just as there was in London? And a Cornhill Street? And what about Duke of Gloucester, King George, and Prince George Streets?

The Sands family and other Annapolitans liked being English. When King George had a birthday, the whole town turned out to celebrate with bonfires near the dock and the firing of the cannon at the battery. Later, men gathered in the public room of the Sands inn to drink toasts to the king's health. At bedtime Nan made sure that her seven-year-old sister, Sarah, and her brother Joseph, who was six, remembered King George in their prayers. And on Sundays the Sands family walked together up Church Street to St. Anne's, which was the Church of England in Maryland.

When Nan went shopping for her mother, the coins she counted out were English shillings and pence. The pewter dishes they ate on, the buttons on the front of Will's waistcoat, Nan's needles and pins, John Sands's carpenters' tools, and almost everything that had to be bought in a store came by ship from England. And, when those ships came in, Annapolitans spoke to their captains and crews in English.

Oh yes, the Sands family and other Annapolitans were English. All they really wanted were the rights of other Englishmen to have a say in what the Parliament did when it was making laws for people in America. By 1774, the government in England had been ignoring the rights of Americans for so long that a small thing like a three-penny tax on a pound of tea was enough to turn the world that the Sands family and other Americans had always known upside down.

Ships stopped coming from England with goods to fill the stores in Annapolis. When Annapolitans went shopping, they found fewer things to buy and more reasons to be angry. At the Sands ordinary, customers still wanted a meal, a bed for the night, or a bumper of ale. But with lemons, limes, and sugar growing scarce, John Sands stopped making his popular rum punch. Nan and Sarah gathered raspberry leaves and other leaves and roots to brew instead of tea. Later, everyone called such concoctions "Liberty Tea," but it wasn't as good as real tea. Americans had to get used to coffee. Its bitter taste reminded people how angry they were at Parliament and King George.

By the end of 1774, people were talking of independence, but some Annapolitans didn't want America to break away from England. They were called Tories or loyalists, and they were not welcome in many places in Maryland. Many Tories had to leave their homes, businesses, friends, and sometimes even families. Anthony Stewart was a loyalist, and he was forced to flee to

England, leaving his family behind. Peggy Stewart, her mother, two brothers, and two sisters went to live with Peggy's grandfather, James Dick. He was her mother's father and a wealthy merchant in London Town, a river port and ferry landing south of Annapolis. James Dick was also a Tory, but he was careful to stay out of politics.

Men in Annapolis were signing up for the militia in case King George decided to send his redcoats to Maryland as he had done to Massachusetts. Bostonians called the red-coated English soldiers "lobsterbacks," but on the Chesapeake Bay, Annapolitans were used to a different kind of shellfish and called them "boiled crabs." In April 1775, news of the Battle of Lexington and Concord reached Annapolis, and the militiamen began drilling in earnest. When he could slip away from chores at home, Johnny went to watch the drills on the field along the Severn River. John Meek, one of the town drummers, was learning to keep time for marching feet, beating out "Reveille," "Assembly," "Quick March," and other orders that foot soldiers had to learn. Fifer Edward George was learning marching tunes.

The shrill voice of the fife and the rat-a-tat-tat of the drum carried all the way over to Prince George Street and the Sands house. In the kitchen yard, Joseph Sands and Davey, son of the family's slaves Hagar and Tom, marched with sticks of kindling as Edward George piped "The World Turned Upside Down."

"Will We Be Fighting Soon?"

That summer of 1775 was hot as usual, and the weather stayed warm all through September. It was good weather for outdoor meetings. Every time you turned around, John Meek or some other drummer was calling people to patriotic meetings under the Liberty Tree, which stood in a field near the top of Prince George Street. Joseph Sands and other small boys listened from the limbs of the big tree or climbed around on the crumbling walls of Bladen's Folly, a mansion started years before by a spendthrift governor.

Winter arrived and with it came rumors that there soon would be British warships on the Bay. Some people were frightened and moved out of town. In January 1776 a boat brought the news that Virginia's Tory governor, Lord Dunmore, had set the town of

Norfolk afire. It burned for two days and destroyed more than nine hundred buildings. Most of the people in Annapolis lived in wooden houses. Many, like the Sands house, were close to the harbor—too close if the British attacked. More people left. Able-bodied men and boys went to work on fortifications around the waterfront. They tested the cannons at the battery.

That same month, a battalion of regular troops in the service of the province of Maryland mustered in Annapolis and Baltimore. Their commander was Colonel William Smallwood, a planter from Charles County. He demanded hard work and discipline from his soldiers and required them always to have a respectable military appearance. Even though they had no real uniforms, Colonel Smallwood ordered the men of his battalion to keep their hunting shirts and leggings clean so that they would look as "formidable as might be." Captain John Day Scott took command of the Seventh Company, which was one of the six companies formed in Annapolis. Another company was organized in Baltimore.

Like many Marylanders, Will Sands did not want to see British troops on American soil to enforce laws in which Americans had no say. If the men of Lexington and Concord were prepared to fight for liberty, the men of Annapolis and other Maryland towns would be, too. On January 20, 1776, Will enlisted in the Seventh Company of the First Maryland Regiment. He was known to be a good shot, a good worker, and a good talker. Although he was only twenty, Will was made a sergeant right away, and Captain Scott sent him out to recruit men for his company.

When he was recruiting, Will was accompanied by John Meek, the company's drummer, and fifer Edward George. Their playing always drew a crowd. Will was ordered to look for able-bodied men who were good marchers, "well practiced in the

use of firearms," and strongly in favor of American liberty. He wrote each name down in his ledger book and then sent the new recruit off to find a gun if he didn't already have one and to get fitted out to go a-soldiering.

"Will we be fighting soon?" the new soldiers asked Will. "Soon enough," he told them.

In February 1776, Maryland's Council of Safety bought a ship they called the *Defense.* They rushed to arm and equip it to protect Annapolis and Baltimore from attack by British warships. Their preparations were none too soon.

The blustery winds of March brought two pilot boats into port with dreadful news. A British man-of-war and two smaller ships were headed up the Bay. The militia prepared for an attack, but they were far from ready. Will Sands was still trying to outfit the men of Captain Scott's company. Mostly they needed bayonets, bayonet belts, and cartridge boxes, and there was never enough gunpowder. Civilians joined the militiamen to defend the town. John Sands carried a musket, but his cartridge case was empty when he took his place behind the breastworks at the harbor's entrance.

On Thursday, March 5, the British sloop-of-war *Otter* passed Annapolis and sailed up the Bay. There, on Saturday morning, it was confronted by the *Defense.* After a two-hour standoff between the two ships, the *Otter* sailed back down the Bay to anchor off Annapolis.

Nan and Sarah; their mother, Ann Sands; the cook Hagar; and Hagar's daughter Eliza worked from dawn to dark preparing food for Johnny and other boys to carry out to the men who stood guard along the town's waterfront. They waited nervously for the boys to return with news.

Shortly after noon on Sunday, Johnny came home with word that the British ship had gone back down the Bay. Later when the men returned, they were jubilant and relieved. If the British had attacked, they would have been powerless against them. They whistled "The World Turned Upside Down" as they marched in a ragged line back to town.

That night, men gathered around the fire in the public room of the Sands ordinary and gave a toast to America and liberty. Just about everybody had unkind words for King George. Upstairs, Sarah and Joseph did not say a prayer for the king, but for a new hero—General George Washington.

Over the summer of 1776, Marylanders put their last colonial governor on a ship back to England and made ready to send troops to join General Washington's army fighting the British in the north. On July 2 in Philadelphia, William Paca, Thomas Stone, and John Rogers of Maryland voted for independence and two days later approved the words that Thomas Jefferson had written. A month later, Marylanders Samuel Chase, Charles Carroll of Carrollton, William Paca, and Thomas Stone joined other members of the Continental Congress to sign the Declaration of Independence. The break with England was official.

While the Continental Congress was debating the issue of independence in early July, Annapolitans were preparing to fight for it. Will Sands's company and the rest of the First Maryland Regiment were ordered north to join General Washington's army. As a sergeant for Captain Scott's Seventh Company, Will made sure that the men had everything they needed to go into battle and were ready to leave. He then got to work on his own equipment to be sure that he presented the respectable military appearance that Colonel Smallwood required. He repaired the worn stitching on his leather cartridge case and the shoulder belt and scabbard for his bayonet. He cleaned his musket and made sure that he had plenty of flints. He was pleased that Nan had mended his hunting shirt and had made him a new linen shirt and overalls. At his mother's urging, he added a warm wool blanket to his bedroll in case the fighting lasted into winter. She also gave him a small Bible to tuck in a corner of his knapsack and strict orders to write at every opportunity. To be sure that he did, she gave him paper and a small writing case containing a sander, an inkpot, a quill holder, and sealing wax.

On July 10, Ann Sands and her children walked to the dock where a crowd had gathered to bid farewell to the seven hundred men of the First Maryland Regiment. One by one, each company lined up to board the sailing vessels that would take them up the Chesapeake Bay to the Elk River. From there, the regiment would march to Philadelphia. Will supervised the loading of the Seventh Company's tools, tents, cooking utensils, and other equipment aboard John Sands's sloop *Hope,* which normally carried freight from one Bay port to another. It was one of six such boats assembled to ferry the troops up the Bay to the head of the Elk River. Will had little time to say good-bye to his family. When everything was neatly stowed away in the hold of the *Hope,* he quickly hugged his sisters and Joseph and reminded Johnny that now he was responsible for bringing in fresh game for the larder.

He turned last to his mother. "Don't fret," he told her, when he saw tears glistening in her eyes. "I'll write at the first opportunity." Then he added, "And I'm sure I will find comfort in my Bible, but I don't expect to have need of a blanket. This will be over before the summer is out."

He turned quickly, waved to his family, and joined the other soldiers on the deck of the *Hope.* John Sands gave the order for Tom to cast off. The town guns fired a salute, and the soldiers and the crowd shouted, "Huzzah! Huzzah! Huzzah!" They were on their way.

On July 20, in Philadelphia, Will took out his writing case and began a letter to his parents.

"Honoured Father and Mother," he wrote, "I Send this Hoping it will find you and all Your Family in Good Health as I am at Present and have Been Since I Left Annapolis . . . we Expect to go from here to New York Tomorrow, and When we Get to the Camp I Shall Write. We are all in Good Spirits . . . Remember me to all Inquiring friends."

He wrote again on August 14: "I send to inform you that I am well and Quite herty as I hope this will find you and all the

Family. Our Maryland Battalion lies Encamp'd on a hill about one Mile out of Newyork where we Lay in a Very Secure Place. There is about 200 Sail of the King's Ships Lay Close By us . . . We are Ordered to hold our Selves in Readyness. We Expect an Attack hourly."

Will did not know that more than four hundred British warships lay at anchor off Long Island. It was the largest fleet ever seen in America. Twenty-seven thousand British regulars and Hessian soldiers were being put ashore.

Of more immediate concern was keeping the American forces together. "We have Lost a Great many of our Troops," Will continued in his letter. "They have deserted from us at Philadelphia and Elizabeth Town and a Great Many Sick in the Ospitals. There is Rations Given out at New York for 6000 men dayley . . . We Expect Please God to Winter in Annapolis, those that Live of us."

"What Brave Fellows
I Must This Day Lose"

Late on Monday, August 26, Captain Scott's company and the rest of the First Maryland Regiment were ordered to Brooklyn, which was across the East River on Long Island. About ten thousand American troops from several colonies were in scattered camps around the island. By the time the Marylanders landed near Brooklyn, night had fallen. In the dim light of lanterns, Will went from one group to another in his company to be sure that all were accounted for, that their cartridge boxes were filled and their powder dry.

"Will we be fighting soon?" the soldiers asked. "Yes," he told them. And he was right.

At three o'clock in the morning, scouts brought word that the British were on the move. Nearly ten thousand seasoned British and Hessian soldiers were advancing on the American positions. William Alexander, a general in the Continental Army, was ordered to take two regiments to stop the British. Because he believed that he was an heir to the English Earl of Stirling, he liked to be called Lord Stirling, and that is what everyone called him. When the general looked around, the two regiments "nearest at

hand" were the First Marylanders and a regiment of Delaware Continentals, a total of about 950 men. Most of them had never been in battle, but when they were called, the Maryland and Delaware men marched boldly into the dark to stop the British.

At daylight in the "red and angry glare" of the sun, Will's company and the rest of the Marylanders formed a line of battle as they had practiced at home on the field by the Severn. With muskets loaded this time, the company stood ready to do battle in true English fashion. The thunder of cannon and mortar fire drowned out the sound of John Meek's drum, and the air was thick with smoke. As cannonballs and mortar shells crashed all around them, the men of Maryland and Delaware stood their ground, waiting for the enemy soldiers to attack. At other places around Brooklyn, the battle was going badly for the Americans. Everywhere, they were in retreat. The sun was directly overhead when the British finally attacked Lord Stirling's men.

The 950 soldiers of Maryland and Delaware were surrounded on three sides by 9,000 British troops. Behind them was a wide salt marsh and beyond it was Gowanus Creek. Lord Stirling's men were not about to surrender. Their only other choice was to retreat through the marsh and swim the creek. At that spot, Gowanus Creek was dangerous to swim. It ran fast and deep and was eighty yards wide, but on the other side, sheltered by a ridge known as Brooklyn Heights, was the rest of the Continental Army, and—for the moment—no British. From their vantage point high atop the ridge, General Washington and his officers could only watch helplessly.

Gowanus Creek was not all that stood between the Marylanders and safety. British General Charles Cornwallis had seized the Cortelyou House on Gowanus Road where he had cannons and troops to fire on the Americans as they waded through the marsh to the creek. The British expected that it would be an easy job to stop them. They did not reckon on the men who made up the Maryland Line.

To save as many men as he could, Lord Stirling decided on a bold and desperate plan. He ordered Major Mordicai Gist and about 250 Marylanders to hold off the British while the rest of his men crossed Gowanus Creek. Maryland's Colonel William Smallwood was with General Washington on Brooklyn Heights, and when he saw the men of his regiment fighting their way through the marsh, he sent two cannons down to the shore of the creek to cover the soldiers trying to swim across.

Captain Scott's company was among the Marylanders ordered to attack the British around the Cortelyou House. The British were surprised when the Americans attacked, but they quickly recovered. Their muskets and cannons roared, and many of the Marylanders fell. From where he watched, General Washington fully expected the small Maryland force to surrender. And they did stop and fall back, but they were not defeated. They charged the house again.

"Good God, what brave fellows I must this day lose," General Washington said when he saw them.

Three more times they charged, and behind them, the rest of the Maryland and Delaware troops escaped across Gowanus Creek. By the fifth assault, Cornwallis's forces were almost ready to give up, but just as the Marylanders rushed the house a sixth time, more British troops arrived. That was the end of the battle. Lord Stirling was captured. Only Major Gist and nine other men managed to fight their way to Gowanus Creek and swim to safety.

That night, when company sergeants went through the camps to count how many had returned, they found only 96 of the original Maryland regiment. Most of the 256 who were unaccounted for were either captured or lay dead around the Cortelyou House and in the marsh and waters of Gowanus Creek. No one knows now where he fell, but Will Sands was among the dead who were later buried by the British in a common grave in Brooklyn.

"Yankee Doodle"

*B*attered and tired, the Marylanders had a short time to rest once they reached Brooklyn Heights, but the Battle of Long Island was not over. George Washington now had fewer than nine thousand men; the British had more than twenty-five thousand. He and his generals decided to save what was left of their army on Long Island to fight another day. On the morning of August 29 they began planning a retreat across the East River to New York. That evening a northeasterly storm brought rain and heavy fog, which in the growing darkness helped to hide Washington's troops as they clambered into boats to cross the river. For the dangerous job of covering the American retreat, General Washington needed soldiers he knew he could depend on. He chose men from Pennsylvania, Connecticut, and those who were left from Colonel

John Haslet's Delaware Continentals and Colonel William Smallwood's First Maryland Regiment. These men were "the pick of the army," and as they stood watch, the rest of the American army slipped across the East River. Shortly before dawn, the last of the troops were on their way to New York. The Marylanders finally could leave their guard posts on Long Island and board boats bound for safety.

Sometime after they reached the mainland, the regiment sent couriers back to Maryland with news of the devastating battle that had killed so many of the colony's young men. In Annapolis, a crowd stood somberly around the door of the Coffee House on Conduit Street where the courier read the list of those who would not be coming home from Long Island. John Sands was there to hear it. Grimly, he carried the sad news home that Will had been killed in the battle.

Nan was in the kitchen with Sarah and Hagar when she heard her mother's cry. The three of them ran into the public room. Johnny and Joseph, who had followed their father in from the street, were already there. They listened to the terrible news and knew in that moment that their world had been turned upside down and would never be the same again. With their arms around each other, Ann Sands and her daughters cried loud and long. Joseph tried to be brave and not cry, but soon he was in his mother's arms, too. Johnny ran from the house, through the streets, and into the woods until he could run no more, and there he let himself cry. If John Sands shed a tear, none saw it.

Will's parents could only hope that their son had been buried and a prayer said over his grave. When she was calm again, Ann dried her eyes with a corner of her apron. She asked her children and husband to draw close to say a prayer for Will and all the others who had died so far from home. In the doorway leading from the kitchen, Hagar stood with Tom and their children. They, too, bowed their heads and added their amens at the prayer's end.

"God's will be done," said Ann. "We are all sensible of our loss and must grieve, but it is of little use for us to spend our time idly in melancholy thoughts."

With a clap of her hands, she sent everyone off to pick up the day's chores where they had left off when they learned that the courier from the north had arrived. Shooing Sarah and Joseph ahead of her, she joined Hagar in the kitchen to begin the evening meal. Their public room soon would be full of men and talk of the Battle of Long Island. They had to be ready to go on.

Nan took her sewing basket and a large piece of black velvet into the kitchen garden to sit under the apple tree and stitch arm bands for her father, Johnny, and Joseph. For herself, her mother, and Sarah, she made black rosettes to pin on their bodices or mobcaps. She tried not to think of the new shirt she had made for Will soaked with the blood of his mortal wound.

There was no time for the Sands family to mourn. The war everyone had been talking about finally had begun and they already knew too well what it could cost. Other families in

Annapolis had lost sons and fathers and brothers, and more able-bodied men soon left to join the army. With so many gone, the men, women, and children left behind had twice as much work to do. Annapolis was a busy supply center, a gathering place for food, clothing, medicines, guns, and ammunition for the soldiers at the battlefront. Along with the ordinary, John and Ann Sands kept a small store. Through it, they supplied the ship *Defense* with salt pork, beef, and biscuits. John Sands sailed the *Hope* from port to port collecting meat, grain, and other foodstuffs for the army. He brought the supplies back to the Victualing Office at the town dock, where they were given out to the hundreds of soldiers who passed through the city on their way to battle. Sometimes, the *Hope* carried supplies from Annapolis down the Bay to be shipped to Maryland troops fighting in the south.

With much of the powder and shot going to the army, Johnny learned to hunt with bow and arrows for meat to put on the family's table. Nan and Sarah were busy helping their mother in the ordinary. Over the summer of 1778, Nan sewed seventy-four shirts and twenty-four pairs of overalls and delivered them to John Muir, who was the Continental Army's Commissary of Stores, at the Victualing Office in Annapolis. Joseph and the slave children, Davey and his sister Eliza, had chores from dawn to dusk.

Nan was seventeen, Johnny was fifteen, Sarah was nine, and Joseph was eight when the war for independence began in 1776. Nearly every day for the next five years—until the war ended with the surrender of General Cornwallis at Yorktown in October 1781—they heard the sound of marching feet in the streets of Annapolis, and sooner or later a fifer would play "The World Turned Upside Down." And it was so. They were not English anymore. By the year 1781, they were calling themselves citizens of the United States of America. Joseph and Davey often followed the marching soldiers through the town, stepping proudly to a new tune. And when they had to leave the soldiers, they whistled "Yankee Doodle" all the way home to Prince George Street.

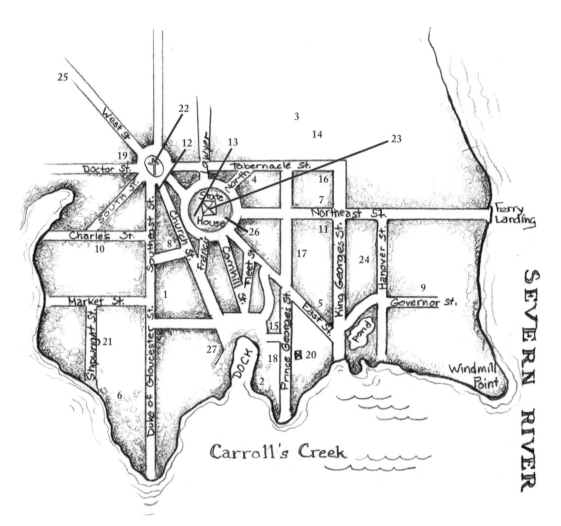

1	Assembly Rooms	8	Coffee House	14	Liberty Tree	21	Scott House
2	Battery	9	Governor's House	15	Middleton Tavern	22	St. Anne's Church
3	Bladen's Folly	10	Green House	16	Ogle Hall	23	State House
4	Bordley House	11	Hammond House	17	Paca House	24	Stewart House
5	Brice House	12	Hyde's House	18	Prison	25	Town Gates
6	Carroll House	13	King William's	19	Reynold's Tavern	26	Treasury Building
7	Chase-Lloyd House		School	20	Sands House	27	Victualing Office

Historical Background

There is much more to the story of the Sands family and the town and the times in which they lived. What follows will tell you about Annapolis, the Sands family, and the Maryland Line and perhaps will answer questions you might have had as you read *The World Turned Upside Down.*

Maryland and Annapolis in 1776

On the eve of the Revolutionary War, Annapolis was a town of about four hundred houses and several large public buildings. It was not as large as Boston, Philadelphia, or New York, but it was an important port and the capital of Maryland. In 1776 carpenters were at work on the roof of the brand-new State House.

The four Marylanders who signed the Declaration of Independence lived in Annapolis. William Paca, who was later a governor, had a stately five-part Georgian town house on Prince George Street. The home of Charles Carroll of Carrollton, who was one of the richest men in the colonies and the only Catholic to sign the Declaration of Independence, stood on a rise overlooking what was then called Carroll's Creek. Thomas Stone bought Anthony Stewart's house on Hanover Street in 1779, and Samuel Chase, who later became a Supreme Court justice, began a handsome three-story house on Northeast Street, now Maryland Avenue, but sold it before it was finished. Others built impressive houses in Annapolis in the years before the Revolution, which brought an end to the city's "golden age." Across the street from Samuel Chase was the elegant house completed in 1776 by Mathias Hammond, who was one of the patriots who urged destruction of the tea brought to town by the *Peggy Stewart.* On East Street was the grand Georgian mansion built by planter James Brice. The homes of Maryland Attorney General Stephen Bordley and Dr. Upton Scott were the earliest of the Georgian-style mansions in Annapolis.

Most Annapolitans lived in much smaller, less grand houses. Some were built of brick but many more were built of wood. Often people did business where they lived, as did Ann and John Sands. Jonas and Anne Catherine Green published the *Maryland Gazette* in the print shop behind their house on Charles Street. Carpenters, silversmiths, saddlers, shoemakers, and other craftsmen had their homes and shops on Francis, Cornhill, and Fleet Streets and along Carroll's Alley.

More shops and taverns lined Church Street from the waterfront to the circle where, in 1776, St. Anne's Church was in ruins. During the war, there was no money to rebuild the church, so its members worshiped in an empty theater building on West Street. The theater hadn't been used for plays since 1774 when the Continental Congress put a stop to such frivolous things. Congress also stopped the horse races, which had been run on a cleared course just beyond the town gates.

The busiest part of town was the waterfront. On one side of the town dock was the Ship Carpenter's Lot. On the other were wharves and warehouses. The harbor was always filled with sailing vessels from near and far. People traveling between the northern and southern colonies used the Chesapeake Bay as a highway. Annapolis was a popular stopping-off place.

Innkeeping was a good business. Benjamin Franklin, George Washington, Thomas Jefferson, and many other important people passed through Annapolis. Sometimes they were entertained by the royal governor, sometimes by friends who had homes in Annapolis. George Washington and Patrick Henry were among those who stayed at the Coffee House, a popular inn on Conduit Street. Another busy inn was Gilbert Middleton's at the town dock. In the late 1770s, many travelers stayed at Thomas Hyde's new three-story inn at the top of Church Street.

A windmill stood on the point of land where the Severn River and Carroll's Creek met. Colonial housewives baked all of their bread, and once or twice a week, they bought fresh cornmeal and flour from the mill.

During the Revolutionary War, Annapolis was an important supply center for the Continental Army. Food, clothing, guns, and ammunition were stored in warehouses near the dock. Thousands of soldiers passed through Annapolis and Anne Arundel County on their way to and from the battlefront. Many buildings, such as the old prison across from the Sands house on Prince George Street, were used to quarter the troops.

Many Marylanders who did not join the army worked at home to help win America's independence. They collected food and other supplies needed by the fighting men and, as a result, Maryland came to be known as the "Breadbasket of the Revolution." Most importantly, Maryland gave many of her men to fight for American independence.

The Sands Family and Their Life in Colonial Annapolis

John Sands was a mariner, and on the eve of the American Revolution, he owned a sloop called the *Hope*. One of the things he did to make a living, besides running an ordinary, was to carry freight on the Chesapeake Bay from its eastern to its western

shore, to Norfolk in Virginia, to the growing town of Baltimore on the Patapsco River, and to the Elk River at the top of the Bay. People paid him to carry wheat, beans, corn, tobacco, beeswax, empty barrels, barrels full of salt meat, wooden staves for making barrels, lumber for houses and boats, feathers for feather beds, letters, messages, and packages of all sorts. When there was room, he even carried a passenger or two.

John Sands bought the ordinary on Prince George Street in 1771. His wife, Ann Sands, helped him run it. At the Sands ordinary, customers could get a hearty but plain meal for a shilling and nine pence. For another nine pence, they could buy a quart of beer. A place to sleep for a night cost them six pence. Ann Sands also sold butter, milk, and eggs, as well as vegetables and herbs from her garden. The Sands family had two milk cows. They kept other cattle and hogs for meat and sold their hides to the tanyard across town. Some of the meat was used fresh, but much of it went into their smokehouse or was salted in barrels to use or sell later. Once or twice a year, John Sands sailed the *Hope* to the West Indies with wheat, corn, or lumber from Maryland and returned with salt, sugar, molasses, ginger, and cocoa to sell in Annapolis.

The Sands family's five-room house was built around a giant chimney. The two upstairs rooms were bed chambers for sleeping. Each of the rooms had a fireplace. Two large rooms downstairs, which also had fireplaces, were public rooms where people ate and drank. John Sands used a third downstairs room as a storeroom for the goods he bought and sold. The kitchen was behind the house in a separate building. Its fireplace was large enough for Joseph to stand in without bumping his head. Outside the kitchen door was a kitchen garden filled with vegetable and herb beds and an apple tree. There, too, was the necessary and beyond that were a smokehouse; pens for chickens, pigs, and the milk cows; and a stable and small paddock where customers could put their horses for a night.

Like many Annapolitans, John Sands owned slaves. Two young men named James and Harry loaded and unloaded cargoes on the *Hope* and helped to sail her. Sometimes they worked on the waterfront for merchants and shipowners who paid John Sands for their services. Harry and James also earned money for John Sands by carrying wealthy visitors and Annapolitans around the town in a sedan chair so that they would not have to walk through the dust or mud of city streets. Another of John Sands's slaves was Tom. He worked on the *Hope,* did carpentry and other jobs for John Sands, and drove the Sands family's horse and wagon. Tom's wife, Hagar, did most of the cooking in the ordinary. They had two children, ten-year-old Eliza and seven-year-old Davey. They slept on pallets in an attic above the kitchen, and there they kept their few belongings. James and Harry slept in the loft over the storeroom.

In addition to travelers, sailors and men who worked around the nearby dock took their meals in the public room at the Sands ordinary. Dinner was served around two in the afternoon. Every morning Ann Sands and Hagar began cooking at dawn and by dinnertime had a hot meal ready. For his shilling and nine pence, a customer might sit down to a meal of stewed beef, venison, roast chicken, or ham. Johnny Sands was a good fisherman, and at almost every meal, there was baked or boiled fish. With the meat, Ann Sands served bread, butter, and cheese; potatoes or corn; and cooked vegetables and salads depending on the season. She usually made a boiled pudding or a pie. Dinner was washed down with beer or cider. Those who didn't want to pay the price for a hot meal could order cold meat from the day before, boiled eggs, bread and butter, and something to drink for a shilling. Whatever food wasn't eaten at dinner was saved for the night's supper or for the next day.

Later, in the public rooms, men gathered to talk, to play card games and checkers, and to drink ale or rum punch. They paid for tobacco taken from a jar on the mantel and for the use of long clay pipes kept in a rack beside the fireplace. Each new smoker broke a piece of the pipe stem off so he would have a fresh mouthpiece.

At six pence a night, a person didn't expect a bed all his or her own. People almost always had to share—usually with another traveler, but sometimes with a member of the family. In the 1700s, working class people almost always had to share a room. Beds could be in any room of a house, even the kitchen. Often when the courts were in session or people were in town for markets and fairs, the Sands family had to put extra beds in one of the public rooms. At the end of the day, customers carried candles to light their way up the curving front stair to a bed. Some nights, their snores rattled the roof timbers.

John and Ann Sands slept in one of the upstairs rooms. Sarah and Nan shared a tester bed in the same room. Will, Johnny, and Joseph slept in the other upstairs bed chamber. If the ordinary had many paying guests and more places were needed in the beds, the boys slept on pallets on the floor of their parents' room. For Nan and Sarah, sharing a bed had advantages, especially in the winter. It was much better to climb into bed, pull the bed curtains, and snuggle down into the feather bed with another warm body. The coals smoldering in the fireplace across the room were not enough to keep them warm. The last thing Nan did before she and Sarah climbed into bed was to fill the bed warmer's pan with a few hot coals and run it between the covers.

Like most children of the working class, the Sands children were expected to help their parents as soon as they were able. They began doing chores around their homes at the age of six or seven. If a boy of eleven or twelve did not go to work with his father to learn a trade, he often was apprenticed to a blacksmith, bricklayer, carpenter, shoemaker, tailor, weaver, shipwright, or someone else who could teach him a skill with which he could earn a living. Sometimes a boy was apprenticed to a person in another town or on a plantation and had to leave home.

While boys learned a trade, girls learned how to manage a household. They learned how to cook and bake, to spin and sew, to make candles and soap, to do laundry and clean a house, to care for children, and to nurse the ill. Sometimes, when a young woman married, she worked with her husband to keep a shop, or

work a farm, or, as Ann Sands did, to run an ordinary or tavern. Nan helped her mother in the ordinary. She did sewing and mending for her family. She stitched hundreds of linen napkins for the ordinary and earned money by sewing for other people in town. During the Revolutionary War, she sewed more than one hundred shirts, seventy-five pairs of overalls, and fifty pairs of trousers for the army.

The Sands children went to school long enough to learn to read and write and cipher. The boys may have attended King

William's School near the State House. Nan taught Sarah to sew and also helped her and Joseph with their school work. Sarah practiced her sewing, her writing, and her arithmetic by making samplers. Nan, whose name was really Ann after her mother, liked to sew. She also liked to read. Among her books was one on Africa, Guinea, and other strange lands, called *A Curious Collection of Travels*. Other books taught her useful things, such as shopping, cooking, and preparing a family budget. One author declared that a young lady must have "a spirit of obedience, pliability of temper, and humility of mind," which might have prompted Nan to write inside the cover of one book:

Ann Sands, her book, her hand, her pen.
She will be good, but God knows when.

Will worked with his father on the *Hope*. He often took the sloop's tiller and, like his father, was able to steer her through the treacherous shallow waters of the Bay and its many rivers. He knew how to make the best use of the cargo space in the sloop's hold, how to keep accounts, and how to bargain with farmers and merchants for the goods his father bought and sold. Will also took care of his father's horse and the horses of the ordinary's customers. Every year when the weather turned cold, he helped with butchering the cattle and hogs and preparing the meat to be smoked or salted. He was a good shot with a musket and kept the household supplied with wild turkeys, geese, ducks, and other birds, as well as rabbits, squirrels, and occasionally deer from his hunting trips.

Johnny fed the family's milk cows, which were pastured behind the house. The other cattle were kept in the public pasture beyond the town gates at the end of West Street. Johnny could find his family's cattle because their ears were notched, or earmarked, in a way that was different from the earmarks of other people's cows. He took care of the family's pigs, which were also earmarked. They were penned near the milk cows' pasture. Johnny preferred the cows because they stayed where they were put, but the pigs were another matter. They were always getting loose, running in the streets, and making people very angry.

Johnny's favorite chore was fishing. In fair weather, he could almost always be found in his skiff on the Severn or nearby creeks. Besides fish, he came back with oysters the size of a man's foot and large diamondback terrapins, which his mother made into a rich soup. He also tended the fires in the ordinary's five fireplaces. Every night Johnny banked the coals with ashes so he would not have to start a fresh fire in the morning. He was out of bed before sunup to rake away the ashes and gradually build up the fire with kindling and logs. With the help of the bellows, he coaxed the glowing coals into flames. The kitchen fire came first so that it would be ready for Hagar to begin cooking.

Sarah helped in the kitchen. She especially liked baking days with their yeasty smell of fresh dough and warm bread just out of the oven. Every day she and Eliza had dozens of iron knives and pewter spoons to wash. Forks were used in only a few of the finest houses in town. The family and customers used pewter plates—exactly sixty-eight of them. Sarah kept a count every week when she polished the pewter with wood ashes and water. Every morning Sarah fed the chickens and collected their eggs. That was her favorite job. Everybody's least favorite job was making soap, but they did not do that often. Ann Sands usually bought soap. It came in a large block, and she cut off pieces as they were needed. The Sands family still made candles, though—dozens of them in large and small molds. Another of Sarah's jobs was to make sure that the candle boxes on each mantel were filled.

One of Joseph's most important jobs was to keep the wood boxes beside each fireplace full. His other big job was fetching water from the town well. He had help with both jobs from the slave boy Davey who was just Joseph's age. They shared most chores. If people could not find one boy, they would start looking for the other when they had errands to be run or water buckets to be filled. Joseph was big for his age and strong from carrying wood and the heavy water buckets. He and Davey had to step carefully between the ruts in the street so as not to slosh the water. If they spilled too much, they would surely have to go back to the well for more.

Joseph Sands was twenty-three in 1791 when his father died. He helped his mother run the ordinary until her death in 1796. He inherited the house on Prince George Street, and when he married, Joseph stopped using his house as an ordinary. Instead, he became a merchant and operated a packet schooner between Annapolis and Baltimore. He had ten children. Nan and Sarah moved into a small house next door when Joseph married. His brother, John, worked in Baltimore for a time and then returned to Annapolis where he became a constable.

Joseph Sands was my great-great-great-grandfather, and today, I live in the Sands house in Annapolis. I spent much of my childhood in the old house listening to stories that my grandmother and great-aunt used to tell about the family and life in Annapolis in days gone by. The past was very real to me because of the house and especially because of the things it contained. The Sands family never threw anything away, and each generation passed along a treasure trove of everyday objects that family members began accumulating before John Sands bought the house in 1771.

To write *The World Turned Upside Down,* I could walk through the rooms the Sands family had used in 1776 and hold in my hands a candle mold, or a bed warmer, or a pewter plate that was in the house then. Before we placed them in the Maryland State Archives for safekeeping, I held the letters that Will Sands wrote from Philadelphia and New York and the yellowing pages of Ann's journal.

Even with these things, I was left with many more questions than answers about the Sands family and their life in Annapolis during the Revolutionary War. They were not famous people. No

one ever wrote about them, and they didn't write about themselves. To tell the family's story, I went to history books, historical records, and historians for the facts that I needed about colonial life in Annapolis. To the best of my knowledge, the basic facts in *The World Turned Upside Down* are true, but at times, I had to use my imagination to create a scene involving Nan or Johnny or Will Sands.

I am indebted to the Maryland State Archives and State Archivist Dr. Edward Papenfuse; the Historic Annapolis Foundation; historians Nancy Baker, Shirley Baltz, Jane McWilliams, Arthur Pierce Middleton, Jean Russo, and Robert Worden; and numerous published histories and other materials.

The Maryland Line

On Long Island in August 1776, the First Maryland Regiment's brave stand enabled George Washington to withdraw his battered army to continue the fight for independence. Today, these Maryland soldiers are known as the "Maryland Line," and Maryland is known as the "Old Line State."

The Maryland Line, which fought throughout the American Revolution, included the eight regiments from Maryland that joined the Continental Army in 1776. Many Marylanders fought with units from other states, but only the regiments of 1776, which were identified as Maryland Continentals, are considered to be the Maryland Line. Because the men of the Maryland Line fought so bravely to win America's independence and because Maryland is one of the oldest states, it has come to be called the Old Line State.

In wars such as the American Revolution, the men of opposing forces usually began a battle in lines facing each other. This was called the battle line. At the time of the Revolution, most of the soldiers had muskets that only fired one shot and then had to be reloaded. As the lines walked forward, the men in front fired their muskets. They then moved back to reload, and the men behind them stepped to the front to fire. This went on until they were too close to shoot, and then they fought with pistols, swords, or bayonets. Even when they did not fight this way, the soldiers on each side in a battle were called a line.

With fresh new recruits from home after the Battle of Long Island, the Maryland Line faced the British again at Harlem Heights and later at White Plains and Fort Washington in New York. Fighting beside men from Delaware and Pennsylvania, they stood their ground against more experienced and often more numerous forces when others retreated. General Washington depended on tested, reliable soldiers like the First Marylanders because they "inspired our troops prodigiously," he said, and could make a dreaded enemy "give way."

By the spring of 1777, recruits had built Maryland's First and Second Brigades up to about twenty-five hundred men. Although Marylanders sometimes accounted for less than ten percent of the Continental Army, they continued to be troops George Washington could count on when he needed men to draw attention away from his main force or to hold the line. They fought at Princeton, New Jersey, in January 1777; at Staten Island, New York, in August 1777; at Brandywine and Germantown, Pennsylvania, in September 1777; and at Monmouth, New Jersey, in June 1778.

Commanded by General Baron Johann DeKalb, the Maryland Line with a regiment of Delaware Continentals marched south to the Carolinas in April 1780. By August they were in North Carolina, and for the rest of the southern campaign were very low on food and most other supplies. At Camden, South Carolina, the Maryland and Delaware Continentals stood with Virginia and North Carolina militiamen against British regulars and American loyalists. When the British charged, the inexperienced militiamen could not hold their positions. General DeKalb and his force of about six hundred Maryland and Delaware troops fought off two thousand British until the baron fell. Wounded eleven times, he died three days later. Losses among the Maryland and Delaware troops were heavy, and the original Maryland Line of 1776 had all but disappeared. Those who remained were formed into a new regiment with new officers in January 1781.

That month, the Maryland and Delaware Continentals, commanded by Lieutenant Colonel John Eager Howard of Baltimore, defeated the British at Cowpens. The Marylanders under General Otho Holland Williams faced the British again in March at Guilford Courthouse in North Carolina. A month later, they fought again at Hobkirk's Hill. Fighting into the fall, they participated in the siege of Fort Ninety-Six and the Battle of Eutaw Springs in South Carolina, both of which kept British forces from reinforcing Cornwallis's troops under siege at Yorktown, Virginia.

In the meantime, General William Smallwood had recruited men in Annapolis to join General Washington's army at Yorktown. Led by General Mordicai Gist, they arrived in Virginia in October 1781. When Cornwallis surrendered on October 19, 1781, George Washington sent his aide-de-camp, Colonel Tench Tilghman of Maryland, to carry the news to the Continental Congress in Philadelphia.

On September 3, 1783, the treaty between the United States and Great Britain was signed in Paris. The men of the Maryland regiments were discharged from the army and by November 1783 were on their way home to pick up their lives again. In Annapolis, Congress was meeting in the Senate Chamber of the Maryland State House. Not only did the members of Congress have the treaty to consider, but on December 23, 1783, they received George Washington's formal resignation as commander-in-chief of the Continental Army. On January 14, 1784, Congress ratified the Treaty of Paris. Seven years of war at last had come to an end.

General William Smallwood

General Mordicai Gist

Notes

Page 12—The tune called "The World Turned Upside Down" was included in William Chappell's *Popular Music of the Old Times,* published in London around 1895. The music appeared first in England in 1643 as "When the King Enjoys His Own Again." It has had several other titles, including "Derry Down." According to legend, the British played "The World Turned Upside Down" when Cornwallis surrendered at Yorktown in 1781. No one knows for sure if that is true.

Page 18—The Church of England, or Anglican Church, was established as the official church of the colony of Maryland in 1692. Marylanders paid taxes to support it, even if they were not Anglicans. After the colonies declared their independence, citizens were free to worship as they chose and no longer supported churches with their taxes. In America, the Anglican Church became the Protestant Episcopal Church.

In addition to English coins, Marylanders used coins from other countries. One of the most common coins was the Spanish dollar, which people often cut into eight pie-shaped "bits" to make change. We still say that a quarter is two bits. Merchants used small money scales to weigh their change to be sure that each bit was actually one-eighth of a dollar.

Ships were not coming from England because Marylanders and other colonists were boycotting British goods as a protest against the closing of Boston's port. The boycott was made official when the Continental Congress passed a nonimportation agreement in December 1774.

Page 20—Except for the names of the Sands family's slaves included in various wills, I know very little about their lives or how they really were related to each other. City records mention that John Sands was a slaveholder and that he was paid for the labor on the wharf of a "negro" named Tom.

Page 23—William Smallwood was not made a general until October 1776.

William Sands and most of the other men of the First Maryland Regiment wore hunting shirts. The Continental Congress did not decide on an official uniform for Continental soldiers until 1779. The hunting shirt was made of heavy white, buff, or brown linen. Most soldiers wore heavy linen ankle-length leggings or overalls. George Washington preferred overalls for his soldiers.

Pages 27–28—John Sands placed an ad in the *Maryland Gazette* to let people know that his sloop, the *Hope,* was available to carry freight.

Pages 28–29—In colonial days, there were few rules for spelling, capitalization, and grammar. Many people spelled words the way they sounded. Notice on page 29 that Will spelled "hospitals" as "Ospitals," which was probably the way it was pronounced at the time.

Pages 48–49—Records in the Maryland State Archives show that John Sands obtained his first license to sell "spiritous liquors" in 1767 and thereafter was regularly licensed as an ordinary keeper.

Items in John Sands's will and inventory offered clues to the contents of each room in the house.

Page 52—In her journal, Ann Sands kept track of how many shirts and pairs of overalls she made and to whom she delivered them.

Pages 52–53—Ann Sands also noted that Sarah and Joseph went to school in March 1775, but she doesn't say where.

Glossary

abed—in bed.

ale—a type of beer.

able-bodied—strong and healthy.

advantage—in battle, having a better position.

aide-de-camp—an assistant to a high-ranking military officer.

apprentice—in colonial days, a boy or young man legally bound to a master craftsman for a period of years to learn a trade.

assembly—a legislative body; the signal for troops to gather and be prepared to march or fight.

at bay—when a person or animal is unable to flee and must confront pursuers.

bank a fire—to cover the coals of a fire with ashes to make it burn slowly without going out.

battalion—an army unit or group of soldiers made up of smaller groups of soldiers called companies.

battery—a group of large guns or cannons; often set up to guard the entrance to a town or harbor.

battlement—a strong wall built of brick, stone, earth, or wood.

bayonet—a steel blade attached to the end of a musket or rifle barrel and used in hand-to-hand fighting.

bed warmer—a long-handled, covered pan filled with hot coals and run back and forth between the covers of a bed to warm it.

bellows—an instrument used to start or increase a fire by blowing air on hot coals to produce a flame.

Bladen, Thomas—a colonial governor who planned an elaborate mansion but could not finish it because the legislature did not approve of his plans and refused to give him more money.

boat hook—a long pole with a hook at the end used to push or pull a boat or to pick up ropes used to tie a boat to a wharf or pier.

breastworks—strong walls built in a hurry to keep out attackers; usually breast high.

brig—a two-masted sailing vessel with square sails.

brigade—a large body of troops.

bumper—a cup filled to the top; often called for when making a toast.

by-your-leave—an apology for not asking permission to do something.

canteen—a small container, usually with a strap, used by soldiers and others to carry water.

cartridge—a long, round case filled with gunpowder; put in a musket barrel along with a small lead ball.

cast off—to untie a boat.

chamber—a room; in colonial times, usually a bedroom.

cipher—to do arithmetic.

clamber—to climb or scramble.

Commissary of Stores—a person in charge of food and supplies for the military.

company—a small group of soldiers; part of a battalion.

concoction—a combination of ingredients.

Continental Congress—the assembly or meeting of delegates from the thirteen American colonies; meetings began on September 5, 1774, to discuss the problems with Great Britain and how to solve them; on July 2, 1776, the delegates adopted the Declaration of Independence; they acted as a central governing body during and after the Revolutionary War.

Continentals—soldiers in the Continental Army during the American Revolution.

courier—a messenger.

course—a place or track for horse racing.

court days; courts—Maryland's county law courts were in session at each county seat for several weeks at a time; in Anne Arundel County, when people came to Annapolis to take care of legal matters, they often stayed for days or weeks to do other business.

Council of Safety—In June 1774 a convention of delegates from every county became Maryland's governing body. A year later, a fifth convention created the Council of Safety as its executive branch to carry out the convention's wishes and to manage the day-to-day business of the province. Among other things, the council was responsible for recruiting men for the militia; fortifying towns; and buying, equipping, and arming the ship *Defense* to protect Maryland from an attack by British ships coming up the Bay.

coverlet—the top covering of a bed.

crown—a unit of British money equal to five shillings.

diamondback terrapin—a turtle with a diamond-shaped pattern on its shell; they are now rare in Bay waters.

drill—to train to march or shoot.

drummer—a town drummer was a man or boy hired to beat a drum to call people to hear special announcements or news. In the military, the drummer's beat helped keep soldiers marching in step, told them how fast to march, sounded the start of the day, called them to formation or meals, called them into battle, or passed other orders to them.

dry goods—woven fabrics, threads, yarns, and similar materials.

Duke of Gloucester—the son of Anne, Queen of England from 1702–1714. He died at the age of eleven.

earl—a nobleman.

embark—to board a boat or ship or to begin a voyage.

fair days—in the spring, fall, and on special occasions, fairs were held when people went to a nearby town to buy and sell farm animals and produce; to compete in wrestling matches, foot races, and other games; to watch gentlemen race their horses; and to attend plays, dances, and other entertainments.

feather bed—a quilt or sack stuffed with feathers and used as a mattress.

ferry—a place where people, horses, carriages, and livestock were carried across a river, creek, or bay; a boat powered by sails or poles or pulled by a rope for crossing a body of water.

fetch—to go for and bring back.

fife—a high-pitched flute used in military and marching music.

fit out—to supply with clothing or equipment.

fleet—a group of ships controlled by one country, state, or person.

flint—a piece of hard quartz that makes a spark when struck by steel.

flintlock—a type of gun in which a piece of flint strikes against steel to make a spark and cause the gun to fire.

folly—a foolish action.

foot soldiers—men trained and armed to fight on foot; infantrymen.

formidable—causing fear and discouraging attack.

frame house—a house made of wood.

fret—worry.

frivolous—not serious or important.

game—wild animals hunted for food.

Georgian—an elegant, symmetrical style of architecture popular during the reigns of the English Kings George I–George IV from 1714–1820.

ground or go aground—when a boat or ship hits the bottom beneath the water or runs up on shore.

gypsies—wandering people once believed to have come to Europe from Egypt. They actually came from India.

half-penny—a coin valued at half a penny; there were also farthings, equal to one-fourth of a penny, and sixpence, equal to six pence, or pennies.

Hessians—German soldiers who were paid to fight with the British during the American Revolution.

hoist—to raise or lift.

hold—the space inside the hull of a boat or ship used to store cargo.

hose—stockings.

huzzah—a cheer.

inkpot—ink for use with quill pens was kept in small containers made of glass, brass, pewter, stone, and other materials that would hold a liquid.

jackknife—a large folding pocket knife.

jubilant—showing great joy.

kindling—a small piece of wood or other material used to start a fire.

King George—George I, heir to the English throne when Queen Anne died in 1714.

knapsack—leather or heavy cloth case for clothes and supplies carried by a soldier or traveler on his back.

larder—a place where food was stored; a pantry.

leggings—pants.

Lord Stirling—actually born in America, William Alexander and his father before him believed that they had inherited the English title "Earl of Stirling," and Lord Stirling is what William Alexander called himself.

man-of-war—a large warship.

mariner—the navigator or captain of a vessel.

Maryland Line—men who fought with the First Maryland Regiment during the American Revolution.

marsh—wet land along the edge of a river, creek, or bay.

melancholy—sad.

militia, militiamen—a group of men called by the government of a colony, state, or nation for military service in times of emergency.

mobcap—a woman's hat, usually worn indoors. It was made of a circle of cloth drawn into a large, bowl-shaped cap by a string or ribbon.

molasses—a thick, dark syrup made from brown sugar.

mortal—causing death.

mortar—a type of cannon.

musket—a heavy, long-barreled gun that fires only one shot at a time.

necessary—an outside toilet.

ordinary—an inn or tavern; typically one used most by the middle and working classes.

packet schooner—a fast-sailing, two-masted vessel that ran on a regular schedule carrying cargo, passengers, or mail.

pallet—a small, temporary bed that can be easily moved.

Parliament—the national legislature of Great Britain.

pence—pennies.

pewter—a combination of tin and lead used to make dishes, cups, and other utensils.

pilot—a person able to guide ships through difficult waters. In Maryland and Virginia, pilots raced out to sea in small, fast sailing boats to help ship captains steer their ships into the Chesapeake Bay. They also helped captains sail safely on the Bay and its rivers, which had many dangerously shallow places.

planter—owner of a large farm, or plantation, used for raising crops or livestock; some of the wealthiest, most powerful people in Maryland were planters.

pocket—a pocket in colonial days was a bag attached to a belt or string, sometimes worn under other clothing for security or because it was soiled. Decorative pockets were worn outside other clothing.

port—a city or town on the water where ships regularly load and unload cargo and passengers.

pound—British money equal to twenty shillings or 240 pence.

powder and shot—the gunpowder and lead ball used as ammunition in a musket.

Prince George—Queen Anne's husband, the Prince of Denmark, but not King of England.

province—another word for colony.

public room—the main room of an inn or ordinary.

quarter—to provide housing for troops; to force a person or town to provide places for soldiers to sleep and eat.

Queen Anne—Queen of England from 1702–1714; in 1695, when Anne was still a princess, Maryland's Governor Francis Nicholson suggested that the colony's new capital city be named Annapolis in her honor and the General Assembly agreed.

quill—the shaft or stem of a feather, which was sharpened and used for writing with ink.

quill holder—a metal, wood, or leather tube for carrying quill pens. Usually only the shaft of the feather was used.

rations—food provided for soldiers.

recoil—to fall back.

recruit—to persuade men to enlist in the army and to sign them up.

Redcoat—a British soldier; so-called because of the color of the uniform.

regiment—a large group of soldiers made up of two or more battalions.

regulars—experienced troops (*see* seasoned troops).

reinforce—to make stronger by adding more soldiers.

retreat—withdrawing from a dangerous situation.

reveille—a signal for troops to get up in the morning.

salt meat—beef, pork, or fish cured or preserved with salt for later use; usually stored in barrels.

sampler—an embroidered piece of cloth showing a beginner's skill in sewing.

sander—a small metal or wooden shaker filled with absorbent sand to sprinkle on wet ink to speed its drying.

scabbard—a leather or cloth holder for a knife, sword, or bayonet.

sealing wax—wax used to hold a letter closed.

seamstress—a woman whose job is sewing.

seasoned troops—soldiers who have been in battle and know what to expect.

sedan chair—a boxlike vehicle with a seat inside for one person, carried on poles by two people, one in front and one behind.

shilling—a British coin equal to the twentieth part of a pound or twelve pence.

Ship Carpenter's Lot—an area set aside near the Annapolis town dock for building boats.

shipwright—a shipbuilder.

shutters—used not only for privacy, but for warmth in winter, to keep a house cool in summer, and sometimes for protection.

siege—an attack on a town or military force.

skiff—a boat small enough to be sailed or rowed by one person.

sloop—a sailing vessel with one mast; very popular on the Chesapeake Bay in colonial days.

smokehouse—a building in which slow-burning fires produced smoke to preserve meat, poultry, or fish.

spendthrift—a person who spends money wastefully.

staves—narrow pieces of wood used for the sides of a barrel or tub.

stitchery—sewing.

subject—a person who is under the control of a king or other authority.

tanyard—a place where animal hides were made into leather.

tar and feather—to punish a person by covering him or her with hot tar and feathers.

tester bed—a high bed with four posts and a canopy or curtains.

tiller—a wooden handle used to steer a boat by moving the rudder from side to side.

tinder—a dry material that catches fire very quickly.

toast—to have a drink in honor of a person, thing, or event.

to cover—to guard someone from attack.

Tory—an American who opposed the Revolutionary War and remained loyal to Great Britain; a loyalist. In some places, loyalists were tarred and feathered or put in jail. Many had to flee their homes. Some loyalists stayed and fought against their fellow Americans. The Eastern Shore of Maryland was a Tory stronghold.

transport ship—a ship used to carry troops and military supplies.

trivet—a metal stand with three legs that can be put over a fire to hold a kettle, cooking pot, or other container to cook or keep the contents warm.

tutor—a private teacher.

undaunted—showing bravery in the face of great danger.

venison—deer meat.

victuals—food supplies.

victualing—to supply with food.

waistcoat—a vest; pronounced "weskit."

Index

St. Anne's Church, 18, 45

Sands, Ann, 25, 27, 28, 38–39, 40, 44, 48–51, 52, 55; John, 15, 18, 19, 25, 26, 27, 28, 38–39, 40, 44, 46–49, 51, 55, 64n; Johnny, 9–10, 12, 13–15, 20, 26, 28, 38, 39, 41, 50, 51, 54, 56, 57; Joseph, 18, 20, 21, 26, 28, 38, 39, 41, 49, 53, 55–56, 65 n; Nan, 7–10, 12–13, 18, 19, 25, 27, 38, 39, 41, 51, 52, 53, 56, 57, 65 n; Sarah, 18, 19, 25, 38–39, 41, 51, 53, 54–55, 56, 65 n; Will, 13–15, 18, 23–25, 27–35, 38–39, 51, 53–54, 57, 64 n

Scott, John Day, 23, 25, 27, 31, 34

Scott, Upton, 44

Senate Chamber, 61

Severn River, 20, 33, 46, 54

Ship Carpenter's Lot, 45

slaves, 49, 64 n

Smallwood, Colonel William, 23, 27, 34, 38, 60, 61, 64 n

Spanish dollar, 63–64 n

State House, 43, 52, 61

Stewart, Anthony, 9–11, 15, 19, 44; James, 9; Peggy, 8–9, 12, 20

Stirling, Lord, 32, 33, 35. *See also* William Alexander

Stone, Thomas, 26, 44

Supreme Court, 44

taxes, 10, 11, 18, 63 n

tea, 10, 11, 13, 17, 19

theater, 45

Tilghman, Tench, 60

Tom, 20, 28, 39, 49

Tory, Tories, 19–20, 21

Treaty of Paris, 61

uniforms, 23, 64 n

Victualing Office, 40, 41

Virginia, 21; militia, 59

warships, British, 25–26, 29

Washington, George, 26, 27, 34, 35, 37, 45, 58, 59, 60, 61, 64 n

West Indies, 48

West Street, 45, 54

Williams, General Otho Holland, 60

Windmill Point, 13, 46

Worden, Robert, 57

"World Turned Upside Down, The" 12, 20, 26, 41, 63 n

"Yankee Doodle," 41

Yorktown, 41